How to Find the Right Network Marketing Company

Charles H. Holmes

www.OnlineMLMCommunity.com

Legal

Copyright Notice

This book and all related materials are © copyrighted 2018 by Charles Holmes. No part of the contents of this book may be reproduced or transmitted in any form or by any means without permission in writing from the author. Any person who does any unauthorized act in relation to this publication may be liable to criminal prosecution and civil claims for damages.

Earnings Disclaimer

All businesses come with some level of risk. Individual results will ALWAYS vary. Every effort has been made to accurately represent this product and its potential. Examples in these materials are not to be interpreted as a promise or guarantee of earnings. Earning potential is entirely dependent on the person using our product, ideas and techniques. We do not purport this as a "get rich scheme." Your level of success in attaining the results claimed in our materials depends on the time you devote to the program, ideas and techniques mentioned, your finances, knowledge and various skills. Since these factors differ according to individuals, we cannot guarantee your success or income level. Nor are we responsible for any of your actions.

Book Details

Published by *Holmes Internet Marketing*
Copyright 2018 / All Rights Reserved
ISBN: 9781731504036

Let's Work Together!

I would like to formally invite you to partner up with me in my MLM Company. It specializes in natural and organic products.

I've gone through each step in this book to evaluate the company, before I got involved. Needless to say, I am very happy and am quickly moving my way up through the ranks.

As of November 2018, I have a team of 2,600+ reps. I've been working with my company for about 22-months and have personally sponsored over 160 people. I'm currently the company's top producer.

If you want to work with a successful mentor, in the right company at the right time, I would like to invite you to take a look at what I have to offer you. To learn more about my business, simply visit my website:

www.StartaFunBiz.com

To learn more about the products, visit my website:

www.ShopwithChuck.com

Your information is never shared or sold. You can unsubscribe at any time, if you decide it isn't a good fit for you.

Also, feel free to send me an email to chuck@onlinemlmcommunity.com, to ask me your questions. I look forward to hearing from you.

Free 7-Day MLM Boot Camp

Want to achieve success in network marketing? If so, I can help you. I've put together a FREE 7-Day MLM Boot Camp that explains the ropes of the business so you can sponsor more reps, build a big team and make more money in the business.

You will receive one lesson per day by email. To request your FREE 7-day MLM Boot Camp, simply go to my website listed below and opt-in to the form in the right column.

www.OnlineMLMCommunity.com

I know you will enjoy it. If you find the boot camp helpful, feel free to share it with your friends and team members.

Table of Contents

Welcome Message..*3*

Part One: Initial Considerations

    Chapter 1: My MLM Story..5

    Chapter 2: Why Network Marketing? 13

    Chapter 3: Is Network Marketing a Good Fit for You? 25

    Chapter 4: Why Finding the Right MLM Company is So Important 32

Part Two: Things to Look for in an MLM Company

    Chapter 5: The Products or Services.................................38

    Chapter 6: The Company's Track Record & Reputation ..45

    Chapter 7: The Compensation Plan 50

    Chapter 8: Training & Systems 59

    Chapter 9: Technology & Tools 63

    Chapter 10: The Distributor Agreement 66

    Chapter 11: The Start-Up & Ongoing Costs 69

    Chapter 12: Timing...75

    Chapter 13: The Company's Financials & Leadership Team 78

    Chapter 14: Meetings, Events, Support & Culture............ 81

    Chapter 15: Retailing vs. Recruiting 86

Chapter 16: International Markets & Expansion 89

Chapter 17: Your Intuition 92

Part Three: Picking a Company & Sponsor

Chapter 18: The 7-Step Process to Pick a Company & Sponsor 97

Chapter 20: What Now? 106

Final Thoughts *109*

About Me *110*

Recommended Reading *111*

Let's Work Together! *113*

Welcome Message

Thanks for purchasing my newest book, *How to Find the Right Network Marketing Company.*

The purpose of this book is to help you find a network marketing company that you can partner up with for the long haul, so you can build a long-term, stable and secure residual income.

I want you to find a company with products or services you are passionate about, that pays you fairly, and offers you a lucrative opportunity, whether doing the business part-time or full-time.

Other than finding the right sponsor to work with, the company you partner with is vitally important.

In this book, my goal is to educate you about the specific things to look for in a network marketing company. I will teach you how to do your due diligence and the process of actually selecting a company, so you can make an informed business decision.

I hope you enjoy the book and I look forward to hearing from you soon. If you want to ask me a question, or connect, just send an email to chuck@onlinemlmcommunity.com.

Thanks again for your patronage and good luck with your network marketing business. See you at the mountain top!

Part One:
Initial Considerations

Chapter 1: My MLM Story

Everyone likes a good story, right? My network marketing success story will definitely inspire you and give you hope.

I grew up in an entrepreneurial family in small-town Maine. As a young child, I watched my dad follow his dream of leaving the "employee" world to start his own business.

He worked at the local paper mill as an iron worker, but he had a passion for buying and selling antiques. He simply wanted to be his own boss, make his own schedule and call his own shots.

For years, I watched him struggle as he pursued his dreams. We were a typical lower to middle-class family. We were by no means rich. We lived in a trailer for a long time until my parents eventually built their own home.

My mom stayed at home and raised my brother and I, while my dad built his business. My mom also did odd jobs to help pay the bills. She was VERY supportive of my dad. She also spent a ton of time with my brother and I. We always felt loved and well cared for.

By the time I reached high school, I figured going to college would be my best option. I also knew I needed self-discipline, purpose, and direction, so I enlisted in the Army Reserve.

After attending one semester of college at the University of Southern Maine, I left for Basic Training and Advanced Individual Training at Fort Jackson, South Carolina. Upon completion of my military training, I returned home to Maine, and decided I wanted to go Active Duty Army.

My first duty assignment was *The Old Guard*, a very famous Army unit. During my time at this assignment, I took night classes and earned my Associate's Degree.

I also decided to become an Army officer. I earned my commission as a Second Lieutenant in May 2000 from SUNY Potsdam, in upstate New York.

How My MLM Career Began

Fast forward a couple of years to March 2002. At the time, I was a First Lieutenant in the U.S. Army, stationed at Fort Carson, Colorado. My co-worker, another Lieutenant, said she had someone coming over to her house to talk about additional ways of making money.

I was always looking for ways to earn additional money, so I agreed to go. A few hours before the scheduled event, I decided not to go, but my best friend (Watson) reminded me that I gave her my word that I would be there, so I went.

At the meeting, another Lieutenant was the presenter. He was dressed up in a blue suit and red tie. He started drawing circles on a dry erase board and talked about concepts such as leverage and residual income.

Needless to say, he was an Amway rep. What I heard and saw that night MESMERIZED me. I loved the idea of change where you shop, help people, find six serious people and you can potentially earn time and money freedom.

I wondered why no one had ever talked to me about ideas like this before. I went home that evening and signed myself up as an Amway® rep.

I was excited. I didn't sleep much for several days. Now, some 16+ years later, I'm even more excited about what our industry has to offer people.

From day one in Amway®, I was "ALL IN." I was very rough around the edges and needed a lot of personal development, but I was committed to the business.

I met with my successful mentor, created a game-plan, shared my why and goals, and then committed to following their team's success system.

I attended every event, followed the training religiously, counseled with my upline and did what I was told to do.

I achieved moderate success in that company and did make some money. I also learned a lot. Looking back, three things really stand out:

1. The power of personal development
2. The power of association
3. The power of written goals

Those three takeaways completely changed my life for the better. My Amway® experience improved my personal and professional life. I am eternally grateful for my Amway® experience.

After about 2.5 years in Amway®, I resigned my distributorship. I was going through a painful divorce and trying to save my marriage.

For the next 10-11 years, I became an MLM JUNKIE. Gosh, I hate to tell people that, but it is the truth.

During that time, I jumped in and out of MANY different network marketing programs.

Some of the companies I worked with include:
1. Amway®
2. Life Force International®
3. Melaleuca®
4. My World Plus®
5. Watkins®
6. Visalus®
7. Send Out Cards®
8. Herbalife®
9. Isagenix®
10. Young Living Essential Oils®

There are many other companies as well. I just don't remember the names.

Please know upfront that ALL of these companies are great companies. I have nothing bad to say about any of them. **The major problem I had was me.**

<u>I simply did not have the right mindset or skill-set to succeed in this industry</u>. I would sponsor a few people, order products for a few months and then move on to something else. Can you relate?

Like most people in this industry, I struggled. I struggled for YEARS; more than 12-years to be exact. Retailing, recruiting and duplication seemed impossible.

No one I talked to was interested. People told me the products were too expensive. People told me it was a scam. Most people I prospected just wanted a job, not a business opportunity. I heard it all.

Had a few simple things not happened, I would no longer be in this industry. Fortunately, I had several breakthroughs that altered my MLM Career. I'd like to take a moment or two and talk about them.

My Breakthroughs

My first breakthrough happened when I learned that the smartest way to build your network marketing business is to leverage your own strengths, talents, and natural abilities.

I learned that almost every top earner in every company did things differently from the other top earners.

Contrary to what you have been told, you do not HAVE to follow your company or team's system to succeed in the business. Yes, it helps to follow their system initially, but at the end of the day, everyone is different. Trying to put a square peg in a round hole never works.

Innovation was important, not duplication. Successful leaders INNOVATE. I learned this from my #1 mentor of all-time, Mark Yarnell.

Basically, he claimed that *successful distributors figured out what they were naturally good at, and then developed a game-plan that aligned with their strengths and talents*. What a concept!

My second breakthrough was when I took the time to learn MARKETING. Somehow, by luck or fate, I stumbled across two guys: Mike Dillard and Dan Kennedy.

Remember those two names. These two guys taught me marketing. In our industry, you have two options:

prospecting and marketing. Prospecting is when you chase people and marketing is when people chase you.

Both methods work great. I know people who are master prospectors and I know people who are master marketers. I chose to be a master marketer, because I didn't want to chase people at the mall or bug friends and family. I wanted interested prospects contacting me first.

Now, I sponsor 10-20 new reps most months, all through marketing. Every single one of these people contacts me first or signs-up on their own without contacting me at all.

My third breakthrough in our industry was when I joined the right company at the right time.

In our industry, timing is everything. You can succeed or fail in ANY company, both established, ground floor, and young companies.

Established companies are very secure and stable, yet most prospects will have PRECONCEIVED notions about the company.

Ground floor opportunities are very risky. Most ground floor MLM Companies don't survive their first year.

Young companies are where the HUGE opportunity is at in our industry (my opinion). Ideally, you want to join a company before it becomes a household name, but after it has worked out its kinks of being a ground floor opportunity.

Study the top earners in EVERY network marketing company; I can almost 100% assure

you that a large MAJORITY of their leaders joined the company before it hit momentum. They weren't necessarily the first people in, but they got in early.

Ideally, you want to join a company that is about three to ten years old, that is growing each year, yet is flying WAY under the radar. That's my thoughts anyway.

All of the previous companies I worked with (except two) were established, older companies. In those examples, I missed the momentum and rapid growth phases.

Basically, I joined too late. With the two exceptions, those companies simply were not the RIGHT company at the RIGHT TIME.

If this sounds crazy to you, look at your company's top 10 earners and then find out when THEY joined the company. Chances are, at least 8 or 9 of those 10 people got in early! Food for thought.

My final breakthrough happened when I acted AS IF I had ONE-MILLION dollars invested in my business. I decided to stop treating my business like some unimportant part-time project, and started treating it like a REAL business.

I took massive action, at least 10x the effort I had put into any other company. Guess what happened? My business exploded.

Quite perhaps the number one mistake I see people in our industry make is treating their business like a hobby.

Do not do that. Pretend you invested your life savings to start your business and you only have one year to earn it back!

Where I Am Now

I found my current company in December 2016. As of this writing, I've been with them about 22-months. In that time, I've sponsored just over 165 people personally and have built a team of around 2,500 people.

My prediction is that within the next 12-months, my team will grow to 6,000 or 7,000 people and within another 2-3 years, I will hit 20,000 or more team members.

What attracted me to the company were the compensation plan and TIMING. The products are also great.

I have taken massive action with this opportunity. The reason my team has grown so quickly here is because it is the right company at the right time.

My goal is to remain in this company for the rest of my life (assuming nothing crazy happens). I want to be like those Amway® guys and gals who have been getting checks every month from one company for DECADES.

All of the struggles were worth it. I wouldn't change anything. I believe that if you follow the advice in the upcoming chapters, you should be able to find the right company at the right time, so you can start right, and not have to do what I did.

Chapter 2: Why Network Marketing?

Why network marketing? This is a question every single adult in the world should ask themselves AND do their due diligence, before deciding the industry is or isn't for them.

First off, <u>network marketing is a distribution model</u>. It's simply a method for distributing goods and services from a manufacturer directly to the consumer.

Network marketing simply bypasses the warehouse, jobber, and other middlemen and allows consumers to buy directly from the manufacturer, either as a retail customer or wholesale buyer (distributor).

People can become a "distributor" for a network marketing company. This allows them to promote the opportunity to others, get a discount on their own purchases, and sell the products for a profit.

Best of all, the company services the customers. The distributors simply refer people to shop directly with the company. The company handles customer service, collects the payment, ships the product, and processes returns.

The business is built through "word of mouth" advertising and distributors are paid on multiple levels of referrals and on their own personal sales.

In many ways, being a network marketer is similar to being an insurance broker or real estate broker. These "brokers' can sell homes or insurance themselves, and earn a commission by doing so, and they can recruit other agents and earn overrides on their sales. I think of that as a win-win situation.

I personally believe this is the best industry in the history of the world. That being said, not everyone else feels the same way.

While some people are passionate about our industry, others are equally passionate about hating our industry. We are definitely a "misunderstood" industry.

Network marketing is not taught at home or in college. Most people have no clue as to what network marketing really is. In addition, many people have preconceived notions about "what they think" it is, even though they haven't deeply explored it themselves.

One of my most trusted mentors once told me that **100% of the population NOT involved in our industry do not understand it, or they would be involved, and 95% of the people in the industry do not understand it, or they would be building it big!**

That is exactly how I feel. In the paragraphs below, I will share 22 reasons you should consider network marketing, regardless of your current profession or situation in life.

1 Inexpensive to Start

Network marketing has a VERY SMALL barrier of entry. With most network marketing companies, you can get started for less than $100.

As I see it, **this is a blessing and a curse**. Because anyone can get involved, we attract a lot of unqualified people. I've also found that most people won't take their business seriously BECAUSE they don't have much money invested in it!

Compare that to a traditional business owner who often invests $50,000 or more just to open a business, and you will understand what I am talking about.

However, for someone who WANTS to own a business, but doesn't have a lot of money to start a traditional business, network marketing is a great option.

How many other businesses can you think of that you can start for less than $100 and have a monthly overhead of less than $100?

2 No Territories

With many businesses, you have a designated territory. If you own a retail store or a local business, you are more or less restricted to making sales to people who are in your geographical location (unless you have an online presence).

Think about a local gas station for a moment. If the gas station is located in Tampa, Florida, it will never sell gas in Augusta, Maine. It just won't happen. It will only sell gas to people in the local proximity.

With network marketing, you can do business with anyone, anywhere in the world. I currently have team members in about 40 different states and about 20 different countries. I can recruit distributors from ANY country our company does business in.

You can too! Best of all, you don't even have to visit those states or countries to sign people up. You can do it online if you want to.

3 Free Mentor

Most business owners do not want to train their employees everything they know because they know that person might become their competition one day!

In network marketing, you get a free mentor. In addition to the person who introduced you to the business, you can also seek out someone in your "upline success team" to help you.

This person is making good money in the business, has lots of experience, AND is more than willing to teach you everything they know, without charging you a dime. How awesome is that?

How can this happen? **The beauty of our industry is that we can only succeed by helping others succeed.** When your mentor helps you make more money, their check also increases.

4 Small Monthly Overhead

I mentioned this in the low-start up cost section, but I need to expand on this idea.

With network marketing, your monthly overhead is dirt cheap; normally just $50 to $100. To qualify for commissions, you agree to purchase a set dollar amount of products each month.

While the average person might complain about having to buy products every month, anyone with entrepreneurial experience understands how powerful a low monthly overhead is.

You don't need a building. You don't need employees. You don't need insurance. You don't need inventory. You don't have utility bills.

Your only real expense is your own personal purchase, which in most cases, you can consume. For example, in my company, I must purchase about $50 to $75 per month in products to be eligible for commissions.
Best of all, I just switch stores, and buy from myself instead of buying my vitamins at a vitamin store.

5 Work from Anywhere in the World

The average small business owner is a slave to their business. They must show up to their physical location every day at a set time and leave at a set time. They have "set" business hours. If their "shop" is closed their business is closed.

Not so with network marketing. You can work from the beach. You can work on vacation. You can work at home on the couch in your pajamas. You can work at the local coffee shop.

As long as you have your cell phone, laptop and internet connection, you are good to go!
This is the ultimate lifestyle business.

6 No Quotas

Most businesses have quotas. Even if they don't have a traditional sales quota, most businesses have to make X amount of sales just to break even and stay in business.

With network marketing, because of the low start-up and ongoing costs, you have no quotas. You can work your business as much, or as little, as you want, and stay in business.

Even if your business doesn't produce much income in a month, you're not out any money because you simply consumed your personal purchase (something you were going to buy anyway).

7 RESIDUAL INCOME

Most people earn a linear income. They work 40-hours at their job and get paid for 40-hours of work. They do it again each week and keep getting paid.

However, if they stop working, or lose their ability to work, they stop getting paid. That might not sound like a big deal until you get fired or sick, then it's a real big deal.

Everyone needs residual income. **$500 to $5000 per month of residual income would be life changing for 98% of the population.**

Residual income is money that comes in month-after-month for something you did one time. Examples of residual income include military and government pensions, social security checks, book royalties, insurance premiums, etc.

Network marketing allows you to create residual income without having to invest a ton of money or hire people.

8 LEVERAGED income

Everyone needs a leveraged income. **Leveraged, RESIDUAL income should be your ultimate goal.**

Many people start a traditional business for the leverage. They know that if they hire a bunch of employees, they can earn a small profit off each employee's efforts. Big companies have a ton of leverage because they have a ton of employees.

Network marketing gives you leverage without needing employees or large sums of capital. You can build up a team of 100, 500 or 5,000 people and earn a small commission off each person's efforts.

I can't speak for you, but I'd rather make 1 percent off one hundred people's efforts than only get paid on my own efforts.

9 Time & Money Freedom

Wouldn't it be nice to really own your life? Wouldn't it be nice to have the time, money and health to do what you want to do, when you want to do it?

The average person gets very little quality time for themselves each day. When you factor in their work responsibilities, family commitments, and outside the home commitments, I'd bet the average person gets less than one hour per day for themselves.

Network marketing gives you the opportunity to create a solid residual income stream, so you can have more time, money and better health.

Network marketing gives you options. **It gives you the ability to truly own your own life,** something everyone should experience.

10 Personal Growth

One of the best things about network marketing is the personal growth. Some people say network marketing is a personal development business with a compensation plan attached to it. I agree.

This is the only industry I've ever been involved with where you are encouraged to grow as a person. You are mentored. You are taught to read books.

You are taught to attend events. You are taught to spend time with people who uplift you and encourage you. You are taught to set goals!

Who you become on your journey to success is the sweetest reward.

11 Recognition

Babies cry for it. Grown men die for it. RECOGNITION. The average person gets very LITTLE recognition at home or from their employer.

In this industry, people get recognized all the time, even for the smallest of things. There are contests, prizes, cash gifts, trips, cars, plaques, free products and hundreds of other things. This is one of my favorite things about the industry.

As the leader of my own team, it's what I enjoy doing the most: recognizing others.

12 Tax Advantages

I am not a CPA. That being said, I do know that having a home-based business will save the average American family several thousand dollars per year in taxes.

Even if you decide network marketing is not for you, make sure you have some type of home-based business.

13 Make Your Own Schedule

After spending more than 15-years in the Army, I realized I was not a morning person. I work best from about 4 p.m. to 2 a.m.

With network marketing, you can set your own business hours. You still have to work if you want your business to grow, but your hours are very flexible.

You can work an hour here, 30-minutes there, etc. As long as you put in time every day, and work smart, you can grow a successful network marketing business.

14 No Employees

I've been an employee and I've had employees. While employees often complain about their employer, I can personally tell you that having employees is a nightmare.

With network marketing, you need ZERO employees. You are an independent contractor with the network marketing company. Everyone on your team is also an independent contractor.

That means you have no payroll. No employee theft. No employee issues. How about them apples!

15 No Billing/Accounts Receivable

If you have ever owned a traditional business, or have an accounting background, you probably know about accounts receivable.

Most businesses hope their customers will pay on time each month, so they can stay in business. Sadly, not all customers pay on time, or pay at all.

With network marketing, there is no billing or accounts receivable. Everything is taken care of by the parent network marketing company. We simply refer people to shop with them and they handle the rest.

16 No Discrimination or Office Politics

If you are a minority or a woman, there is a good chance you face discrimination in the workplace.

Not so in network marketing. What you do with the opportunity is totally up to you. It doesn't matter if you are young, old, fat, thin, pretty, ugly, white, black, religious, non-religious, smart or dumb.

It doesn't matter where you went to college, what your blood line is, or where you grew up. You don't have to play office politics, kiss butt, or worry about who likes you.

This is a true "equal" playing field. The only thing that matters is YOU.

17 No Commuting

Depending on where you live, I bet there is a high likelihood you sit in traffic every morning and every evening, on your way to and from work. Most people do. Some people love commuting and sitting in traffic. I personally hated it.

Network marketing really can be a home-based business. I drive very little every month and spend my days working from home, with my wife right next to me. My commute is about 30 paces from my bedroom to office. That sure beats sitting in traffic.

18 Condense Your Work Career

In today's world, the average person is going to be in the work force for close to 50-years, if not longer. That's a LONG time.

With network marketing, you really can condense your work career. Although there is no guarantee of success, it is possible.

In just a few short years, you have the potential to build up an asset that continues to pay you for decades to come.

Does your job offer you that? Does your traditional business offer you that? Work hard for a few years and then slow down or stop, but keep getting paid? I doubt it.

19 Fulfilling Work

Everyone should have a job or career that they love. Life is too short to do something you don't enjoy.

Network marketing is very fulfilling. What I love most about this industry is seeing other people step out of their own comfort zone and do things they normally would never do.

I enjoy helping others improve their health, quality of life, and financial situation. I love seeing people grow, develop their skills and learn new things.

20 Choose who You Work With

Ever have a boss or co-worker that really annoyed you? Most of us have.

With network marketing, we get to choose who we work with. If you don't like someone, don't recruit them! If a customer is constantly annoying you, fire them, and go find a new customer. You get to build your own success team and work with whoever you want to!

21 Help People

I don't know about you, but to me, the purpose of life is to serve people. In this industry, the more people you serve and help succeed, the better you do in the business!

If you are a servant leader, and enjoy helping others, I can't think of a better business model to participate in. You can mentor and coach people, watch them grow and help them improve their quality of life at the same time.

22 Build a Financial Legacy for Your Family

Wouldn't it be great to build something that would continue to pay your family, even after you die? In most network marketing companies, you can "will" your business to a loved one.

There are many people in our industry who have passed away, but left a constant stream of residual income to their loved ones. To me, that's one of the greatest gifts you can give your family.

Final Thoughts

There you have it folks. These are 22 reasons you should consider network marketing. I hope you will put some serious thought into your decision and at least give our industry a serious look. I think you will love what you find.

Chapter 3: Is Network Marketing a Good Fit for You?

Contrary to what you might have been told, network marketing is not a good fit for everyone. Being an entrepreneur is not a good fit for everyone.

Some people simply do not have the desire, hustle, skills, or willpower to have their own business. And you know what? That is perfectly ok. We are all wired differently and we are all on a different journey in life.

Before you join any business, (or even start a new career) you need to put some serious thought into whether or not it is a good fit for you.

Here are a few considerations to think about before you get involved with network marketing, or start any business of your own:

Is Your Spouse Supportive?

If you are married, you want your spouse to be supportive of your new business venture.

Guess what? Most spouses have different personalities. Opposites attract. Before you start a new business, you need to sit down and have an honest heart-to-heart conversation with your spouse to see what they think about it.

You don't have to agree with them, or do as they say, but you should respect their input and listen to their concerns and questions. Let them know WHY you want to start your own business. Share your goals and dreams with them and ask your spouse to be supportive, or at least neutral.

Make sure they realize that you want their support, even if they don't plan on building the business with you. If they are still negative, and don't want you to start your own business, after you have shared your dreams and goals with them, then you must decide what you will do.

Will you go against their wishes, if they are negative, and do the business anyway? Or, will you give up and throw in the towel? Only you can decide what to do.

From my own personal experience, I can tell you that it is VERY rare to have both spouses excited about the business. Of all the people I have ever worked with in the past, maybe in 1 in 100 cases were both spouses excited about the business.

That being said, it's not the norm! In almost every case, one spouse is very excited and the other is very negative.

What Are Your Skills?

We all have different gifts. We all have different natural talents and abilities. We are all wired differently from each other.

Before you start ANY business, think about what you are naturally good at. What types of things do you excel in? What activities do you enjoy? How do you like to spend your time? Take the time to sit down and write out your twenty best skills.

To succeed in network marketing, it would really help if you had good:

- Time Management Skills

- Leadership Ability
- Communication Skills
- Teaching Ability
- Sales & Marketing Skills
- An Openness to Learning
- Strong Work Ethic

Don't worry, all of these skills can be learned. Most people joining our industry do NOT have ALL of these skills mastered when they first join, so don't worry about it.

Because we are all wired differently, there are different business models (or jobs) that would be a good fit for each of us, based upon our skills and personality.

What Are Your Goals?

Most people have never sat down and written out their goals for their life. If you're one of those people, I hope you will take the time to do that as soon as possible. It will be a life-changing experience.

Spend some time and figure out your life's purpose, your true calling. Only you know what is best for you.

Depending on what you come up with, you might see that network marketing is a good fit for you. On the other hand, it might not be a good fit for you.

My greatest calling in life is to live an adventure, to learn something new each day and to help people. That's my life's purpose. I shared this with you to give you an example and to help you identify your own life's purpose.

I chose network marketing because it aligns with my life's purpose. It allows me to do the things that are important to me.

And even if network marketing does not align with your life's purpose, I guarantee you it can FUND whatever it is you want to do!

Will It Hurt or Help Your Current Career?

Only you can answer this question. Will network marketing help or hurt your current career? Based upon your current career goals, will network marketing move you closer to your career goals or further away from them?

Some careers are much more demanding than others. Also, if you are 100% passionate about your current career, and can see yourself doing it for the rest of your life, why not just focus on that?

On the other hand, if you don't have a career, or if you hate what you do, network marketing might just be the perfect fit for you.

From my own experience, I've found that the skills I developed during my time in network marketing helped me immensely in my career. The skills you learn via network marketing will benefit most careers.

Do You Really Want to Be Your Own Boss?

Not everyone is cut out to be their own boss. Most people who join our industry quickly figure that out.

Very few people have the self-discipline to manage their time effectively and manage their own schedule.

Yes, the idea of being your own boss initially sounds sexy, but at the end of the day when you have to manage your own time, get things done, and pick up the phone to call prospects and set appointments, it can be downright overwhelming for some people.

To clarify, there is NOTHING wrong with being an employee. Most people are VERY happy being an employee. That's great. We need great employees.

While I love working for myself, and couldn't imagine ever working for someone else, I know most people are not wired that way. Most people simply want a good job with good benefits and job security, and nothing more.

You need to put some serious thought into this question and decide for yourself if you really want to be your own boss.

Can You Go Six to Eighteen Months Without Making Money?

Whenever you start a new business of any kind, there is a steep learning curve. You have to invest your time and money to find clients, learn the ropes, make sales, develop your skills and generate a profit.

From personal experience, most businesses I've owned took me six to eighteen months (minimum) to make any type of profit.

Most of my friends who are serious entrepreneurs will tell you the same thing. No business is designed to just have money flooding in from day one.

Every business requires a learning curve. Every business takes time to get established.

The beauty of network marketing, because of the low start-up and ongoing costs, is that you can be profitable from the first month. Just don't expect it.

Do not look at your network marketing business, or any other business, as an immediate solution to your current financial problems. No matter what type of business you start, it will take time to get it established and profitable. This isn't the lottery.

Also, network marketing is designed to do PART-TIME, and provide additional INCOME. It's best to work the business part-time until you create a full-time income.

Is There a Better Alternative for You?

You won't hear many network marketers talk like I do. Yes, I love the industry, but I am an entrepreneur first. One of the most important questions you can ask yourself is this:

"Is there a better alternative for me than network marketing?"

You do have other alternatives such as dog sitting, selling stuff on eBay®, blogging, working a part-time job, babysitting, consulting, investing in real estate, and hundreds of other things. It's different strokes for different folks.

I suggest you brainstorm at least five potential things you could do to make extra money, before you decide to go with network marketing. That way you can be objective and weigh the alternatives.

The Most Important Questions

- Can you really see yourself as an entrepreneur?
- Will starting a part-time network marketing business help or hurt your career?
- What does your spouse or significant other think about you starting your own business?
- Is there a better alternative to make extra money than network marketing?
- Do you need money TODAY, or can you patiently hold out for 6 to 18-months while you build up your business?

My Best Suggestion

Put some serious thought into whether or not entrepreneurship and/or network marketing are right for you. It is a good fit for some people and a bad fit for others.

Only you know what is best for you. If you are flat out broke, secure a full-time job first. If you are looking to create legitimate tax deductions and create a long-term residual income, consider network marketing.

Final Thoughts

Once again, network marketing is not for everyone. Only you can decide how you want to spend your time and how you want to make a living.

I recommend you make a list of several different ways to make money and then pick the one that works best for you. If you decide MLM is for you, great. If not, no worries. It's your life. Live it to the fullest.

Chapter 4: Why Finding the Right MLM Company is So Important

I have done a lot of dumb things in this industry. Learn from my mistakes.

Over a ten-year period of time, I worked with more than TEN different MLM Companies. I'm not bragging, because I'm not proud of it.

Looking back, I've learned two valuable lessons from that experience that I wish I had known then. What are those lessons?

First off, no company is easy to build. **All network marketing companies require you to put in the work CONSISTENTLY, over a period of several years, to build up a successful business.**

Next, it's easier to start your business right than it is to start over. It makes more sense to put in the time and effort to find the right company to begin with, rather than joining something because you are excited, only to quit a few months later.

I can't even begin to imagine how well off I would be today had I picked the right company, right from the start, and stuck with it for the long haul! Oh well, hindsight is 20-20. Learn from me!

Chances are, you won't pick the right network marketing company the first time around. After all, you don't know what you don't know.

Most people I know who are successful in our industry have worked with several different companies before finding their forever home. That's okay.

However, wouldn't it be great to find your forever home right from day one? It is possible, but you need to do your due diligence first.

Here are the reasons why you want to find the right network marketing company to work with right out the gate.

It Takes Time to Build Up a Stable, Solid Residual Income

No matter what network marketing company you join, it will probably take you three to five years to build up a full-time income, assuming you work your business part-time.

Yes, you can do it faster, but I do believe this is a conservative timeline for success. To some folks, that might sound like forever, but I think it's a great deal. The time will go by anyway.

Considering you keep your day job to pay your bills and work your network marketing business part-time, ten to twenty hours a week, that is actually quite amazing!

Every Time You Start Over You Lose Momentum & Credibility

Sometimes things happen. I get it. There are lots of things in this industry (and in life) that are completely out of our control.

Companies shut down, merge, or change their compensation plan. Lawsuits happen. People get divorced. And countless other things.

There is nothing wrong with starting over. Many of us do that in life. The problem with starting over is that you lose all the time and effort you invested into your business.

You lose momentum. And in some cases, you lose credibility with the people you know and worked with.

If You Do It Right the First Time You Will Make More Money

Most of the really successful reps in this industry have been with their company for at least ten to twenty years. Folks, that's a long time.

When you pick the right network marketing company, you won't need to jump ship. You'll find something you can stick with for many, many years.

In most cases, your business will grow and mature each year, which will cause your income to grow. Once you have a rock solid, stable team, life is really good.

Remember, it takes a while to build up a large residual income. When you start over, you have to begin all over again.

That's not fun or easy. There might be times when it is necessary, or makes sense, but you should try to avoid it at all costs.

Find the right network marketing company from day one, and stick with it the rest of your life. That should be your goal.

It's Hard to Start Over

When you start over in a new network marketing opportunity, you have to go out and sponsor a lot of people again, to find your key leaders. Chances are, most of your former team will not follow you to your new company.

Starting any new business requires a ton of work. It's much easier to maintain and steadily grow a business than it is to launch a new one.

The Most Important Questions

- How certain are you the company is stable and positioned for long-term growth?
- Can you see yourself spending 20, 30 or more years affiliated with this company?
- Does the company's culture and values align with your own beliefs?

My Best Suggestion

Start slow and start right. Don't just jump into any business opportunity because of excitement or hype. Start right the first time around so you don't have to start over.

Act as if you are investing one million dollars into your MLM Business and do the required research to find the right opportunity for you.

Final Thoughts

In summary, starting right is much easier and better than starting over. Put a lot of time and thought into the network marketing company you pick. Do your due diligence and be an educated entrepreneur!

Part Two:

Things to Look for in an MLM Company

Chapter 5: The Products or Services

Everything, and I mean everything, starts with the products or services. *If the products don't make sense, neither will the business.* That's how I see it.

What I want to share in the paragraphs below are different things to consider when you evaluate a network marketing company's products or services.

Your Passion Toward the Products

Do you love the products? Are you excited to share them with others? Would you still buy them and use them even if you weren't involved with the business?

If you can answer YES to those questions, you are headed in the right direction. I believe it is vitally important to be passionate about the products or services you will represent. Some people might disagree with that, but I believe it's important.

When you are passionate about something, your passion shines through when you talk with other people. If you aren't passionate about the products or services you represent, you won't have the conviction in your voice when you talk with other people!

You can't fake passion. Besides, why would you want to promote a product or service you don't really love or use yourself?

Try to find a product or service that sets your world on fire. Try to find something you love so much you think about it all the time and want to tell everyone about it. If you feel that way about the products or services, you are definitely moving in the right direction.

Consumable

You want a network marketing company with products that are consumable, used up, and need to be reordered again, month-after-month. This creates an ongoing demand and residual income.

I have nothing against one-time use products. I just don't see them as a good fit for network marketing.

Your ultimate goal is to build loyal, long-term customers and distributors who reorder the products or services month-after-month, year-after-year.

The only way to make that happen is to find a network marketing company with mass market, consumable products at fair prices.

Mass Market Demand

To me, it is essential that you pick a product or service with MASS MARKET DEMAND. You want something that appeals to the masses, not some small niche group of people.

I understand unique products are very sexy; however, if they are only used by a very small segment of the population you are wasting your time.

By all means, be a customer and use those unique products, but if you're looking for a network marketing company to promote, <u>you need products with mass market demand</u>.

Ultimately, you want products that people already buy and consume on a regular basis. You want something that is a NECESSITY, not a luxury product.

Here is one thing to remember about necessity items: people will keep buying them, even if the economy gets bad.

Not so with luxury items. If things get tough for people financially, the first thing they will do is cancel their auto-ship for those luxury items.

However, if the product or service is a necessity, such as a cell phone bill, electric bill, makeup, shampoo, or toothpaste, there is a much higher likelihood people will keep reordering it.

Price Comparison, Quality & Value

It should be common sense to assume that the products or services must deliver a high value and be of great quality.

Do the products do what they say they are going to do? Do they offer a good deal to customers, even at the suggested retail price?

Would you pay the suggested retail price for the products if you weren't involved with the business opportunity?

That is the million-dollar question. If not, look for a different network marketing company to represent.

Here's what you need to realize. Most people are on a budget. Money is tight. People like to price shop. If they can buy a similar product to what you are selling for 90% cheaper somewhere else, they will not buy from you (and rightfully so).

Most network marketing companies have products that are WAY overpriced. That's why you need to shop around. Do some price comparisons before you join any network marketing company!

Your company doesn't have to have the cheapest priced products around, but they do need to be priced competitively, and in the same ballpark to what you might find at the grocery store or chain store.

Backed by Independent Research

Are the products backed by research? If so, what type of research?

Most MLM Companies have doctors, advisors and medical professionals on payroll to endorse their products. That's cool. You just can't take everything they say at face value, especially if they are paid to endorse it.

Ultimately, you want products or services that are endorsed by a reputable independent third-party. You want products that are INDEPENDENTLY RESEARCHED, tested and verified.

You need to thoroughly evaluate these research reports, to see who they are funded by and also to check the credentials of people making the claims.

Uniqueness

I am not a huge fan of unique products, although some people are. I figured I would include this section, if nothing else, so you at least consider it.

I believe you want products or services that have mass market appeal; however, there are some virtues to unique products that can't be purchased anywhere else in the marketplace.

I am not against unique products, if and only if, they have mass market appeal.

Private Label or Manufactured in House

One consideration about the products or services are whether they are actually manufactured by the MLM Company or not. Many network marketing companies private label their products.

This means that a manufacturing company makes the product and then the network marketing company buys it from them and sticks their own label on it.

I am not totally against this concept. If the product is great, that's fine. If the company has private label products, you have to remember that there are probably a number of other companies in the marketplace who put their label on the same products your network marketing company does.

Availability

Here's one more consideration that very few people in our industry ever talk about. Are your company's products for sale on Amazon® and eBay®? If so, are there lots of products available, or just a few?

Here's what happens. Lots of people who quit MLM want to unload their remaining inventory. After they quit the business, they list their excess products on Amazon® or eBay®.

When they do this, they typically "dump" their inventory at a heavily discounted price, simply because they want to recoup some of their money.

Most network marketing companies prohibit distributors from doing this, but after they quit the company, there isn't much the network marketing company can do about it.

Here's how I see it. If you can find your company's products on Amazon® or eBay® at a discounted price, so can your prospects. Why would a prospect buy it from you if they can get it online for a fraction of the cost?

Although this is out of your control, try to find a network marketing company that doesn't have a lot of products for sale on third party websites, especially eBay® and Amazon®.

Money-Back Guarantee

This tip isn't specifically about the products, but the company you partner with needs to have a rock-solid money back guarantee. People need to have confidence that they can get their money back if they are unhappy with their purchase.

Ultimately, you want a company that has a no questions asked, 30 to 180-day money back guarantee. Most companies in our industry offer a similar type of return policy, although it will vary from company-to-company.

The Most Important Questions

- How passionate are you about the products or services?
- Are the products a good value for customers, even at the suggested retail price?
- Do the products have mass-market demand?
- Are the products for sale on a large variety of other websites at a highly discounted price?
- Do the products come with a money back guarantee?

My Best Suggestion

<u>Always start out as a customer first</u>. Even if it costs you more money initially, try out some products first, to see if you are a satisfied customer. If you aren't happy as a satisfied customer, it makes no sense to become a distributor.

Final Thoughts

There you have it folks. These are some of my best tips on how to evaluate a network marketing company's product line.

I hope you will go through this list when you start evaluating companies to join. Go through each one of these things to see how the products stand up. If nothing else, it will give you added insights and perspective that you might not have considered before.

Chapter 6: The Company's Track Record & Reputation

To me, **reputation is everything**. I've found that good news travels fast, but bad news travels even faster!

Before you join a network marketing company you need to check their track record and reputation online. Why? Because your prospects will.

Don't be scared about what you will find. You need to do your own research so you can see the good and bad about your company, so you can make an informed decision.

Here are some things to consider.

How Long Has the Company Been in Business?

I am not a fan of start-up network marketing companies. Yes, some people are. That's cool. I understand all network marketing companies were start-up companies at one point in time.

That being said, most new network marketing companies fail. I get emails about new ground floor opportunities every single day and in almost every case, these new companies don't survive their first year in business.

I like companies that have been around at least three years, but aren't a household name yet. If everyone has heard the name of the company before, you've probably missed the boat, and are too late in the game.

Yes, you can join an established, well known network marketing company and still succeed, but it's tough. Most of the top earners in every company joined the company before it became a household name.

As a rule of thumb, look for companies that are between three and 10-years old.

Ratings with Better Business Bureau® and Direct Selling Association®

What type of rating does the network marketing company have with the Better Business Bureau®? How many complaints are there? What are the complaints? Research it for yourself. Your prospects will.

Is the company registered with the Direct Selling Association®? Why or why not? If they aren't currently listed, were they at some point in the past?

What other professional associations or organizations does the company belong to? What type of endorsements and reviews have they received from these third-party organizations? Please do your research. Once again, most of your prospects will.

Track Record of the Company's Leadership Team

Personally, **I think it's vitally important to evaluate the company's leadership and management team.** You should look to see if they have an advisory board for the company's distributors.

Also, do the owners have any prior experience as distributors themselves? What are their values? What is their background experience? Do they have a criminal record?

These are important things to research. I understand a company's leadership team can change at any time. I also understand companies are bought and sold all the time.

Even still, do you research and find out everything you can about the company's leadership team and management team.

Ultimately, you want a company that is distributor friendly. And, you want experienced leaders at the helm!

Online Reputation

What is the online reputation of the company you are thinking about joining? Are there thousands of pages of negative reviews online, none, or just a few?

Are there websites set up entirely to talk about the negative things about your potential company? If so, tread cautiously.

Are these websites true? Maybe. Maybe not. Anyone can post their opinion on the internet. For the most part, it is unregulated.

Remember, your prospect will go to Google® and type in the name of your network marketing company (and your name) after they meet with you. If all they find is thousands of pages of negative stuff, they will NOT partner up with you.

Yes, there will always be some negative stuff. That's fine. Everyone has the right to express their opinion.

But, if all you find online are hundreds, even thousands of pages and websites with negative stuff about your company, chances are, some of it is true!

I encourage people to read all of the negative information as well, and look for trends. See if people are all mentioning the same issues. If so, there probably is an underlying issue.

Ask 100 People

I like to call this the acid test, the voice of reason. Take the name of the network marketing company you are thinking about joining and say its name to 100 people. See what type of reactions you get. **What do people say to you? How do people look at you?**

This will give you a quick test to see what others think about the company. I call it THE VOICE OF REASON.

Here's what you need to know. If you say the name of your company to 100 people and they all say "pyramid" or "scam" or they run for the hills, or they give you a crazy look, find another network marketing company to work with.

You don't want to work with a company where everyone has negative preconceived notions about it. You don't want to work with a company where you are scared to tell your prospects the name of your company.

Ultimately, you want a network marketing company that most people have never even heard of before. Just my two cents.

The Most Important Questions

- What is the company's reputation online?
- What are the most common complaints against the company?
- When you say the name of the network marketing company to others, what is their reaction?
- Is the company brand new, past its prime, or on the verge of greatness?
- What can you find out about the company's leadership team and owners?

My Best Suggestion

<u>Think like your prospect</u>. Put yourself in their shoes. Find a company with a good reputation. Look for a company that is a few years old, but isn't a household name yet. Be cautious about joining a start-up company.

Final Thoughts

Reputation is everything (to me anyway). Before you start ANY type of business you definitely want to research the people and businesses you will be working with. You want people with integrity, who do the right thing and do what they say they are going to do.

Most businesses have some negative reviews online. That's okay. Take it at face value. But, if you find tons of complaints and scam pages about the company you are thinking about joining, find a different company to work with.

Chapter 7: The Compensation Plan

I'm assuming you joined network marketing to make money. That's why most people get involved!

If you want to make money, it's important to find the right compensation plan. The compensation plan isn't the only factor, but it should be one of the top factors when selecting a company.

Let me start by telling you that there are several different types of compensation plans in our industry. The most common ones include:

- Breakaway
- Binary
- Matrix
- Unilevel

Here is a very brief overview of each compensation plan, although it will vary slightly by company.

Breakaway – In this type of compensation plan you can sponsor as many people as you want on your first level. Your goal is to go wide and sponsor as many people as you can, as quickly as you can.

As people on your team achieve success, their volume "breaks away" from your volume and you start earning a percentage of their total volume, only if you maintain certain levels of volume yourself. These plans are very lucrative if you are good at recruiting.

Many of the older network marketing companies use this type of compensation plan.

Matrix – With this type of compensation plan you have a limited number of spots on each level of your organization. You can still sponsor as many people as you want, but you are limited to where you can place these people on your team. A popular matrix plan is the 5 x 7.

In this example, you have 5 people on your level 1, 25 people on your level 2, 125 people on your level 3, etc.

The major benefit of the matrix compensation plan is that other people are placing people on your team (which you get paid on). The major downside is you are limited on the number of levels you get paid on.

Binary – At the present moment in time, this seems to be the most popular type of compensation plan in the industry. With the binary plan, you build two teams, a team on your left and a team on your right.

On your first level, you only have two positions, then four on your second level, then 8 on your third level, etc.

The major benefit of this type of pay plan is that you create synergy and have people working together, since you are placing people under other people. The major downside is that it often creates a welfare mentality on your team where people expect you to build their business for them.

I personally HATE the binary compensation plan, because I believe it's not a good deal for the part-timer or little guy.

Unilevel – With this type of compensation plan you can put everyone you sponsor on your first level (just like the breakaway).

There are no limitations. Go wide. With these plans, you normally only get paid 3 to 5 levels deep, and in some cases, you can earn additional "leadership" or "infinity" bonuses as you move up through the ranks.

If you are a good recruiter, this is a great compensation plan. I believe this plan is lucrative for part-timers (just my opinion).

Once again, this is just a brief overview of the most common types of compensation plans in the network marketing industry.

Personally, *I don't believe that all compensation plans are created equal.* Most people will preach that their company has the best compensation plan, but you really have to do your due diligence and crunch the numbers yourself. Talk is cheap!

Here are the most important things you should look for in a compensation plan, as I see it.

Personal Ordering & Retail Requirements

No one ever talks about this, but this is vitally important to me. Look at the company's compensation plan and see the monthly purchase requirements you have to buy yourself each month, just to be qualified for commissions. That number might just blow your mind.

For most companies that number will be anywhere from $50 to $200 per month, just to be eligible for commissions. In addition, <u>check to see if that requirement goes up as you move up through the ranks</u>. **In most companies, it does.**

This isn't necessarily a bad thing, but it's something you should know about ahead of time.

Also, check to see if you can make retail sales instead of having to buy the products for personal use. Some companies will count your personal retail sales in lieu of your personal order, and some companies don't.

Also, check to see what type of retail requirements the company has. Some companies require you to have 5-10 retail customers each month, just to get paid your "team" commissions. Make sure you check!

Average Order Size

The next thing I like to look for in a company is the average order size per person. In other words, on average, how much money does each active distributor and customer spend each month?

In some companies, that number might be $40. In other companies, it might be upwards of $300 per person. It varies a lot from company-to-company.

Why does this matter? Because the larger the average order size per person, the fewer people you need in your group to reach your income goals.

For example, 100 people each ordering $100 per month in products is the same volume as 250 people each ordering $40 per month in products.

Active Rate & Retention

You might not be able to find this statistic out from the company itself, so you will need to ask around.

What percentage of the distributors are active each month? In my own experience (disclaimer) I've found the active rate to be anywhere from 20 to 30 percent of the distributors.

I've talked with many other successful distributors and most of them have told me about 30 percent of their team is active in any given month.

This means that if you have a team of 1,000 distributors, at most maybe 300 of them order in any given month.

This is a VERY important statistic to know. Do not overlook it. Ask around. Most people won't tell you the truth because they believe it will scare you off (or they don't know the answer themselves).

You also want to look at retention. In other words, how many months, on average, do people order before they stop ordering? To me, this statistic really tells me how much people like or dislike the products.

Most people will quit doing the business within their first year, but if they keep ordering the products because they want to, you know the company has great products.

Find out the answers to these questions before you get involved with any company.

Wholesale-Retail Markup

Does the company offer a wholesale-retail markup? If so, what percentage is the markup? I believe that a 20 to 25 percent markup is very generous.

Here's another thing to consider. Are the products still a good deal for customers at the suggested retail price? Or, could they go shopping somewhere locally and find a similar product for 80 to 95 percent cheaper?

You want products priced fairly, even at the suggested retail price. *If it isn't a good deal for the customer it's not a good deal for you.*

How Often Do You Get Paid?

Most companies in our industry pay their distributors once per month. The only compensation plan I've found to pay their reps weekly is the binary compensation plan.

I personally don't have a problem with getting paid once per month, although many people are accustomed to getting paid weekly. If getting paid weekly is important to you, look for a company that offers that option.

Also, check to see how much it "costs you" to get paid. Most companies charge reps a fee just to pay them, whether it be by check or direct deposit.

Numbers to Reach Your Income Goals

If you get nothing else out of this book, spend some time and "think about" what I am saying in this section.

Take the time and figure out how big of a team you need to reach your income goals with your network marketing company. Take into account the active distributor rate, average order size, and payout percentage.

Let me give you a hypothetical example, just to get you thinking. Let's assume you work with ABC Health Products (fictional company).

You want to earn $5,000 per month with the company. In this company, the active distributor rate is 25%, the average order size is 100 points per person, and you get paid based upon the points.

On average, you get paid 5% of your total team's volume. On a side note, from what I have found, this is the approximate payout for the industry, although it does vary slightly by company.

In this example, here is what you would need to do to accomplish that $5,000 per month goal.

- $5k per month in commissions equals
- 5% of 100,000 volume points
- To get 100,000 volume points you need 1,000 distributors each ordering 100 points per month
- To get that, you need 4,000 distributors on your team (since only 25% are active in any given month)

Compare these numbers with three of four different network marketing companies and compensation plans to see for yourself. The results will be mind-blowing.

Ultimately, you are looking for a company with great products you enjoy AND a company where you don't need tens of thousands of people to earn a full-time income.

I would also compare a few different compensation plans to see what amount of volume and team size you would need to earn $500, $1,000 or $2,000 per month.

Most people joining the company are part-timers, and you will want to be able clearly share these numbers with them.

How Much is Actually Paid Out?

What percentage of the company's total revenue is paid out in bonuses? From what I've studied in the industry, that number is normally somewhere between 35 and 42 percent.

No company can pay out 100%. They have overhead and expenses just like any other business. That being said, you want a company that rewards its distributors fairly, while still having products that are priced competitively.

Earnings Disclaimer

Print off the company's income disclaimer and study it. There is a lot of valuable information on it.

Some disclaimers even show the average time and number of people someone sponsored to reach that rank.

You will also find out the average earnings at each rank of the compensation plan. This is all valuable information to know.

Incentives, Trips & Bonuses

Does the compensation plan offer rank advancement bonuses, cash prizes and trips? Does the company do a good job with promotions and incentives to stretch distributors out of their comfort zones?

Some companies do a great job with incentives. Other companies don't do anything at all. I believe it's important to find a company that offers some type of incentive. People love contests, paid trips and extra bonuses. It's very appealing.

The Most Important Questions

- What is your monthly personal ordering and retail requirements?
- What is the average order size for people in the company?
- What percentage of distributors are active in any given month, and what is the retention rate?
- What is the wholesale-retail markup on the products and is the suggested retail price competitive with non-MLM products?
- What size team do you need to have to reach your income goals?
- What percentage of total sales is paid out in bonuses and commissions?
- What types of incentives, one-time bonuses, and trips does the company offer?
- How often do you get paid?

My Best Suggestion

Run the compensation plan under a fine-toothed comb. Do your due diligence. Compare at least three different compensation plans. Evaluate each category I talked about in this section and see what you come up with.

Final Thoughts

In conclusion, not all compensation plans are created equal. It's your job to find a network marketing company that rewards you well for your results.

Chapter 8: Training & Systems

The next thing to look for in an MLM Company is the training and systems.

Systems and training are vitally important in any business. That's one of the reasons franchises are so successful. *Although network marketing is not a franchise, you will want to run it like one!*

Training

Let's start with training. Here are the basic things I would look for:

Getting Started Training – Is there a manual, an introductory call, a webinar, or a series of videos that you can use for your getting started training? You want something simple and effective to use with your new team members.

Weekly Training – Is there a weekly training call, webinar, or live event people can attend to find out about newest updates, and to be part of a community?

Regional Events & Convention – Are there large events where hundreds, even thousands of distributors can attend to learn new things, hang out with other reps, and get motivated?

Training Website – Is there a company training website with standardized training for new reps? If so, how often is it updated and what type of information is on it?

Training Tools – Are there training tools available for purchase? If so, are they priced reasonably?

These things all vary by company. Some companies are actively involved in training their independent reps.

In other network marketing companies, the field leadership does it. I think it's good to find a company that offers a balance of both.

Here's another consideration. How much does the training cost? **I don't like the idea of companies and reps making money off other reps just to train them.** I don't think it's unethical to do that, but I do think it's stupid!

If there is a cost for training, it shouldn't be done for a profit. **The only profit should be made through the legitimate movement of products and services.**

Systems

The system is the solution. I learned that from Michael Gerber, author of "The E-Myth Revisited" and I believe it to be true.

What type of systems do you need? Fortunately, not much. Here is what I would look for:

<u>Lead Generation System</u> – What does the company teach for lead generation other than working your warm market? How do team members generate leads? What type of lead generation systems are in place, are they available for everyone, and at what cost?

<u>Follow-Up System</u> – What type of follow-up system does the company offer its reps to stay in touch with their prospects and team members? There should be some type of contact manager or back office that lets

you manage this. It should be free or priced inexpensively.

Training System – How does the company or upline train new team members? Is it standardized? Is it effective? Is it done live or locally?

Additional Consideration

Do you get black-balled if you want to do things your own way? In other words, are you allowed to deviate from the system and training at all, or will your upline team stop working with you if you try to do things your own way? Be sure to find out.

The Most Important Questions

- What type of training does the company provide?
- What type of training will your sponsor or upline provide?
- What lead generation, follow-up and training systems are in place?
- How much do the training and systems cost?

My Best Suggestion

Check out the system and training BEFORE you join the network marketing company (if possible).

See if you can take a sneak peek at it. At a bare bones minimum, ask your potential sponsor about their systems and training. Have them go into detail and explain everything in as much detail as you need to get your questions answered.

Final Thoughts

You want a company and sponsor with rock solid training and systems. Even if you don't need it yourself, most of your team members will! Find something simple that works and don't deviate. Make sure everything passes the common-sense test.

Chapter 9: Technology & Tools

We live in a digital world. That will not change anytime soon. All business owners, regardless of their industry, need tools and technology to leverage themselves and work smart.

Some network marketing companies are cutting edge with their tools and technology. Most aren't. Before joining any network marketing company as a distributor, here are some things you should evaluate:

Corporate Website – Take a close look at the company's corporate website. How does it look? What type of image does it present?

How about the ease of use? Does it look modern or look like it was designed in the 1990s?

Realize your prospects will visit the website and check it out themselves. You never get a second chance to make a first impression.

Replicated Website – How do the company's replicated websites look? Do they have a lead capture system in place? Are they easy to navigate? Is it easy to sign up or place an order? Does it provide enough information, without being overkill?

Back Office – How does the back-office look? Does it give you access to your team and prospects? Is it easy to navigate? Does it give you the information you need to make good business decisions?

Contact Manager - What type of contact manager does the company provide? Does it allow you to email people easily? Can you track the status of each prospect and know where they are in the follow-up process?

Apps – Does the company have a website that is mobile friendly? Are there apps you can use on your smart phone to make sharing the business and products easier for you?

Business Cards, Flyers & Brochures – Does the company have catalogs? Are they helpful, professional looking and priced fairly? Are there other tools such as brochures and flyers you can order or print off to promote the products or business opportunity?

Promotional Items – Does the company offer shirts, hats, buttons, bumper stickers, sweatshirts and other promotional items with the company's name and logo on it? Are these items good quality and priced fairly?

Evaluate your prospective company in each of these areas. If you aren't happy with what you find, talk with your sponsor and/or upline and see what they have available.

Tools and technology will make your life easier!

The Most Important Questions

- Is the company's website professional and easy to navigate?
- Is the replicated website easy to navigate, easy to place an order and sign up on?
- Are there plenty of business tools available for free or for purchase?

My Best Suggestion

Check out the company's technology. Go through the website and evaluate it in each one of these categories. Have your sponsor show you what the back office looks like and see what is included.

Navigate through the contact manager as well, and see how that works. Finally, figure how much all of it costs and ask yourself if it is a good value.

Final Thoughts

Technology is here to stay. Look for a network marketing company that embraces technology and wants to grow with it, not a company that is old school and stuck in the past.

Chapter 10: The Distributor Agreement

Not all distributor agreements are created equal! While you might be an independent contractor, some MLM Companies want complete control over you.

Some companies even have 50 to 60-page distributor agreements that are so overly complex, you need a lawyer to interpret it. I can't speak for anyone else, but I personally think that's crazy.

Here are some of the basic things you should look for in a distributor agreement.

No Compete Clause

Does the company have a no compete clause? Does it prohibit you from joining multiple MLM Companies? This would be a show stopper for me. I couldn't work with a company that wanted to control me like that.

Internet Marketing Policies

As I mentioned in another chapter, we live in a digital age. Some MLM Companies are still stuck in the caveman days.

If your company prohibits you from building your business online, find another company.

Be sure to read the internet marketing policies in great detail to find out what you can and can't do. If you want to build an MLM business online like I do, you want an internet friendly company.

You will quickly discover that most network marketing companies have strict policies that prevent you from using internet marketing.

Advertising Policies

Take some time and read the company's advertising policies. What can you do and what can't you do? Be sure you have a clear understanding before you sign your name to the dotted line.

Easy to Understand

Is the distributor agreement easy to understand? How long is it? Some distributor agreements are 50 to 60-pages long. It's a confusing and crazy contract that few people in their right mind would sign if they actually read it.

I believe a good distributor agreement should be short and to the point, and written in a way that average people can understand.

Waiting Period

Does the company have a waiting period? In other words, if you terminate your relationship with the company, do you have to wait six to 36-months before you can join another network marketing company?

Believe it or not, many companies have a waiting period. Read the agreement and find out for yourself.

These are just a few things to look for in a distributor agreement.

The Most Important Questions

- Is there a no compete clause?
- Can I participate in more than one company?
- Is the distributor agreement simple and easy to understand?
- Do the internet marketing and advertising policies make sense to me?
- Is there a waiting period if I quit the company before I can join another company?

My Best Suggestion

My best suggestion is to read the distributor agreement closely. Take your time. Make a list of questions and run them by your lawyer, or the company itself, until you get answers that satisfy you. Only sign the distributor agreement if you are okay with the terms.

Final Thoughts

I'd bet that 90 percent of all distributors have never even read their distributor agreement. That is a big mistake as I see it.

Act as if you are investing one-million dollars in your MLM Business. Read the contract, get your questions answered, and make sure you know what you are getting yourself into.

Chapter 11: The Start-Up & Ongoing Costs

What I want to cover in this chapter is the start-up and ongoing costs for your MLM Business.

Please know upfront that ALL businesses require money to start, maintain and grow. This is not a free meal ticket or the lottery. You get out what you put in.

I am a big believer in being smart with your money, but I am also a big believer in investing in your business. Don't be a cheap skate! It does take money to make money.

Start-Up Costs

The real beauty of network marketing is the low start-up cost. It's one of only a few business models I can think of where you can get started for less than a few hundred dollars.

That is a blessing and a curse. *Most people in our industry don't treat their network marketing business seriously because they don't have much money invested in it.*

It's easy to quit the business when you only have $100 to $200 invested in it. To most people that is chump change.

As I see it, this low barrier of entry is the # 1 reason people quit the industry. When you have little money invested in your business it's easy to throw in the towel when things get tough.

I can assure you that a traditional business owner who invested her life savings to start a business will do everything and anything to make her business a success. Not so with most network marketers.

In our industry, most companies offer some type of "starter kit" in addition to the sign-up cost. This ranges in price from a few hundred dollars to a $1,000 or more.

I have never been a huge fan of having someone spend $1,000 or more just to get involved with an MLM company, although I do see the merits of it.

After all, when people invest $1k or more to start their business, there's a good chance they will treat their business more seriously than if they invested nothing.

Some people could consider these start-up kits as frontloading. I don't consider a starter kit frontloading, but I am against people purchasing a large inventory with their initial order.

The real beauty of a starter-kit is that it will introduce the new distributor to the products, give them a <u>small</u> inventory to sell, and hopefully encourage them to treat their new business seriously.

It also allows their sponsor to earn a decent fast-start commission.

On the other hand, I don't believe in having distributors ordering several thousand dollars' worth of products to sell. That last thing I want to see is someone with a garage full of stuff they can't sell. That's one of the reasons our industry gets a bad reputation.

As a rule of thumb (in my opinion), a $200 to $500 starter kit is perfectly fine.

Monthly Overhead

All businesses have a monthly overhead. These are ongoing costs just to stay in business.

If you understand business, you will realize how awesome network marketing is. Other than your monthly auto-ship, you have a very small monthly overhead.

I can't think of many businesses where you only have $100 to $200 per month in overhead. It's actually pretty awesome.

Most traditional businesses have several thousand dollars in monthly overhead expenses, if not more.

Listed below are some of the common ongoing expenses in your network marketing business. Before you join a company, it would be in your best interest to compare the expenses in several different MLM Companies, just to put things in perspective.

Auto-Ship

What is the monthly buying commitment? For most network marketing companies, it is somewhere between $50 and $200 per month.

Assuming you enjoy the products, and you can replace products or services you were already using before you joined the business, with your MLM Company's products, it's a great deal. You're basically just switching stores.

A lot of folks complain about auto-ship. What they don't realize is that most of their living expenses are also on auto-ship. This includes their house payment, cell phone, insurance, electricity, car payment and more.

Replicated Website

Most network marketing companies charge somewhere between $10 and $30 per month for a replicated website that you can use. I know my company gives you a website and back office for free, but most companies don't.

Back Office & Contact Manager

Cutting edge MLM Companies have a good back office and contact manager where you can manage all of your prospects and team members in one place. With most companies, this cost is included with your replicated website, but in some companies, it might be an additional charge.

Training

Some network marketing companies do live weekly training events. Most cost money to attend. I'm not a huge fan for paying for weekly training. No, I'm not cheap. I just believe this should be provided by the company.

If you do have to pay for it, it should be a small fee simply to cover the cost of the venue.

Business Support Materials

Some network marketing companies sell business tools and business support materials. This might include books, tapes, CDs, prospecting magazines, seminars, voicemail services, and countless other things.

I believe these support materials are good; however, they should be sold at cost (or close to it) and exclusively by the company, not by an upline.

If your upline is trying to sell you a bunch of business support materials for a profit, I would personally be concerned.

The only way your upline should make money off you is by helping you move products and services, not by selling business support materials.

Yearly Renewal Fee or Membership Fee

Most network marketing companies charge somewhere between $20 and $100 for your yearly renewal fee. This makes no sense to me. It's just another revenue stream for the company. I would look for a company with no yearly membership or renewal fee.

The Most Important Questions

- What is the start-up and ongoing costs?
- Is training available and for free, or at a fair price?
- How much is the monthly auto-ship requirement?

- Are business support materials available for purchase from the company and are they priced reasonably?
- If your upline is promoting business support materials, do they profit from it?
- Is there a yearly membership fee to be involved in the company?

My Best Suggestion

Evaluate all of the start-up and ongoing costs with the business. Look at each expense and determine if it is a fair deal for you. Is the company giving you what you need to build your business, or are they just trying to nickel and dime you to death?

Final Thoughts

In summary, all businesses have start-up and ongoing expenses. That is okay. It's just your job to be fiscally prudent and do your research to make sure that you get what you are paying for.

Chapter 12: Timing

Timing is crucial when you join a network marketing company. Ideally, you want to avoid start-up companies (high risk), and you want to avoid companies that have been around a long time and everyone knows their name (saturated).

Of course, you can make money working with either an established company or a start-up company. Plenty of people do.

I also realize all network marketing companies were start-up companies at one point in time, and had to work through their growing pains.

I've seen lots of new start-up MLM Companies open for business. Most of them don't survive to their first birthday.

Every time I hear the word "ground floor opportunity" I am skeptical. To me, the last thing I want to do is work really hard for a couple of years with a start-up company, only to have it go out of business.

While established network marketing companies are good (they've proven themselves), they can be saturated. To clarify, saturated doesn't mean bad. It just means that everyone has heard of them.

You could still join an established MLM Company and do well for yourself, but you will have to work much harder than the successful people in the company who joined the company at the right time. *Once again, timing is everything.* **You want to join the right company at the right time.**

When is the right time to join a network marketing company? I would say somewhere between year two and year 10.

The first couple of years in business are usually experimental and risky. Network marketing companies have to work out the kinks and figure out what will work and what won't work.

Normally, companies that survive figure this out in the first few years.

Once a company has made it through the start-up phase, worked through the kinks, and had some consistent growth, that's when you want to jump on board.

That's when you can buckle down, work hard, and ride the momentum all the way to the top.

Look at most MLM Companies in the marketplace objectively and you will quickly discover that a large percentage of their leaders joined sometime during the first two to ten years, before the company hit momentum and critical growth.

The Most Important Questions

- Is the company a start-up? If so, what type of experience do the owners have launching new companies?
- Has the company hit critical growth yet and passed the momentum phase?

- Have most people heard of the company before?
- Is the company still a good opportunity or is it saturated in the marketplace?

My Best Suggestion

Be cautious about joining a start-up company and be cautious about working with a network marketing company that is saturated, and everyone knows about. You want to get in the right company at the right time. Timing is everything.

Final Thoughts

In conclusion, **most successful leaders in our industry joined the right company at the right time.** While start-up companies sound sexy, they are quite risky, and have a high failure rate.

On the other hand, most established, big companies are saturated and have already gone through the momentum phase. Look for a company between two and ten years old that everyone doesn't know about.

Chapter 13: The Company's Financials & Leadership Team

It takes money and good leadership to start and build a successful company in any industry. Network marketing is no different.

Before joining an MLM Company, you should evaluate the company's financial situation and leadership team, with scrutiny.

This might sound extreme, but if you were starting a franchise you would do this. Do it with your network marketing business, just like you would with a regular business.

Let's get started by talking about the finances.

The Finances

At the end of the day, there are really only two types of companies in our industry: privately owned and publicly owned companies. There are merits and downfalls to both.

Privately owned companies do not have to report their earnings publicly, whereas publicly traded companies are highly regulated. Personally, I like privately owned companies.

I feel like publicly traded companies might have stronger financial backing, but they also have stockholders and a board of directors to report to.

Check out the company's financial situation online. Look at their revenue for the past ten years. Is it on the incline or decline?

If the company reports their earnings, look at the financial reports for the past few years and look for trends.

The Leadership Team

The next thing to evaluate is the company's leadership team. Learn what you can about the owners of the company, the President or the CEO, the Chairman of the Board, etc. Here are some questions to ponder:

- What is their past experience as a CEO?
- What other jobs have they held?
- How long have they been involved in the industry?
- Do they have any criminal convictions?
- Are they moral, ethical and honest?

Whoever is running the company, they need to be distributor friendly. Ideally, you want to find a company with leaders who have previous experience as a distributor themselves. This keeps them grounded and distributor focused.

Trust me, **you want a company that is distributor focused!** The last thing you want is a bunch of bureaucrats who don't give a flying crap about the field leadership.

Once again, a lot of companies in the network marketing world really mess this up.

Make sure the company has leadership in place that is distributor friendly, and competent. I understand leadership changes from time-to-time and you don't have control over that, but do your due diligence.

The Most Important Questions

- Is the company a start-up? If so, what type of experience do the owners have starting new companies?
- Has the company hit critical growth yet and passed the momentum phase?
- Have most people heard of the company before?
- Is the company still a good opportunity or is it saturated in the marketplace?

My Best Suggestion

Be cautious about joining a start-up company and be cautious about working with a network marketing company that is saturated, and everyone knows about. **You want to get in the right company at the right time.** Timing is everything.

Final Thoughts

In conclusion, most successful leaders in our industry joined the right company at the right time. While start-up companies sound sexy, they are quite risky, and have a high failure rate.

On the other hand, most established, big companies are saturated and have already gone through the momentum phase.

Look for a company between two and ten years old that is flying under the radar.

Chapter 14: Meetings, Events, Support & Culture

This chapter will cover one of the most common things that network marketers overlook.

Please remember that network marketing is a WARM MARKET business. It always has been and always will be.

Meetings, events, culture and support are vitally important if you want to build a business that lasts.

Look at any of the BIG network marketing companies, and distributors with big teams, and you will see they have these things in place.

Without them, you will not succeed long-term in the industry. Consider yourself warned.

Meetings

Meetings are the lifeblood of your business. You want to partner with a company, and sponsor that has meetings.

Examples might include:

- Launch Parties
- Team Training
- One-on-One Coaching
- Weekly Calls
- Webinars

Ask some questions with your potential sponsor and find out what they do for meetings.

1. Do they have a weekly opportunity meeting?
2. Do they have a monthly training or nuts and bolts meeting?
3. Will they be willing to meet with you and your prospects one-on-one?
4. Do they offer webinars or conference calls?

This is not an all-inclusive list, but it is a good starting point.

Events

Events are really powerful. Example events might include:

- Monthly Rally
- Training Events
- Once a Month Party or Get Together
- Team Trips
- Webinars
- Weekly Calls

Events offer social proof for your team members. Events are where people make the decision to build a big business.

Support

Most new network marketers need a lot of babysitting, handholding and support. Very few people will just take the bull by the horns and run with it.

Find out what type of support is offered by your sponsor, the upline team members and company.

Find out about:

- Coaching
- Mentoring
- One-on-One Training
- Weekly Calls
- Game Planning Sessions
- & More

Most companies won't have 100 percent of these things in place, but they should have some of them in place.

Culture

You want a company with a strong culture. You want a company with a sense of community. People want to feel like they belong to something bigger than themselves.

Companies with a strong culture normally do very well. If your company doesn't have a culture, you'll need to create a team culture yourself, which is a big task.

It's much wiser to work with a company where there is a team culture already in place.

Examples might include:

- Dress codes
- Jargon and saying
- Team or Company Values

This might sound weird to people outside of network marketing, but I would argue that we all want a strong culture.

Think about sports for a moment. People have a favorite team. They wear their team's jersey. They have friends who like the same team.

When they meet a stranger, who happens to like the same team they do, they have an instant bond. That's culture! You want the same thing in your MLM Company.

The Most Important Questions

- What type of meetings are available, how often and at what cost?
- What type of initial and ongoing support will I receive?
- What type of events does the company and upline offer?
- What type of culture does the company have in place?

My Best Suggestion

Please take the time to evaluate the meetings, support, events, and culture the company and upline offers. This might not be critical for you, but you will want these things already in place to help your team.

Final Thoughts

In summary, meetings, events, support and culture are vitally important to your long-term success in network marketing.

At the end of the day, you want a strong culture and community, so you can learn, grow and feel like you are part of something much bigger than yourself.

Chapter 15: Retailing vs. Recruiting

The next thing that I really look for in an MLM Company is the retailing versus recruiting aspect.

This is another one of those gray areas that very few people ever talk about.

If your business only talks about recruiting distributors, I would tell you to look for another company. If the only people in your business using the products are the distributors, I would tell you to look for another company, because you're probably participating in something illegal, or something that's borderline illegal.

In all network marketing businesses, there should be more customers than distributors. There should be a big focus on acquiring customers not just recruiting.

Once again, some companies simply tell their people, "consume the product yourself and recruit people for the business opportunity." To me, that is bad advice.

You want a network marketing company where everyone is taught to build up a solid customer base of at least two to five customers, in addition to building a team of distributors.

For every distributor on your team, you want to have two or more customers, and you want each of your team members (distributors) to have several customers themselves.

If people outside of the business are not using the products, I don't believe the company will last long-term.

Once again, you want a product-based company that focuses on getting customers in addition to team building. <u>Every legitimate business in every industry has customers.</u>

Many companies in our industry do not talk about this aspect of the business, and I think it's a shame.

If you study the top 10 biggest network marketing companies in our industry, they all have a strong retail component, and there's a good reason for that.

That's why they stick around for the long haul, and that's why they turn into really big companies. Without customers, there is no business.

The Most Important Questions

- Is there any emphasis on retailing products?
- Is there training on how to retail products?
- Does the company and key leaders ever mention retailing when they talk?
- Does the company's business presentation mention retailing?
- Is there are a requirement to maintain a certain level of retail customers to be eligible for commissions?

My Best Suggestion

Look for a network marketing company that understands the importance of retailing products, in addition to recruiting.

Interview successful distributors, check out the company's training videos and visit the company's website to see what the "company's stance" is on retailing vs. recruiting.

Final Thoughts

In conclusion, you want to look for a network marketing company that is balanced between retailing and recruiting, not one that is just focused on recruiting.

One of the best things to look for is the quality, uniqueness, and price of the products or services at the retail price.

If the products are so expensive at the suggested retail price that no one "not" doing the business would buy them, I suggest you look for a different company to join.

Chapter 16: International Markets & Expansion

Let's face it; we live in a global economy. There are more than 7 billion people in the world (and growing).

Your network marketing company should do business in multiple markets. The more countries your company does business in, the better.

You want to be able to sponsor people in different countries and build a global team. If your company only does business in one country, you are really limiting yourself.

It doesn't mean the opportunity is bad, if it is in only one country, but if I had to choose between two different companies, and everything else was equal, I would pick the company that does business in many different countries.

The Sign-Up Process

One of the most important things to look at is the sign-up process. Some companies make it difficult to sponsor people internationally.

They create restrictions like you have to be at a certain rank in the company to sponsor internationally, or you have to register a separate account in every country your company does business in.

That is absolutely crazy. You want a company with a seamless sign up process for the new recruit, and the recruiter.

Qualifying in Different Countries

Another thing some network marketing companies do is count your international volume separately. Rather than have all of your volume count for qualification purposes, they make it so you have to qualify at a certain rank in every country you have team members in.

This is also crazy, and downright stupid in my opinion. It's just another way for the company to avoid paying you commissions.

All of your volume, regardless of which country it is generated in, should count toward your qualification purposes.

Shipping

This is another thing that can really limit your international growth. If your company only ships products from the USA, to other countries, it can be very expensive for your international team members.

When you factor in customs, tariffs, exchange rates, and international shipping, in many cases it doesn't make sense financially, for an international prospect to join your team as a customer or distributor.

Find out if your company has warehouses abroad, in different countries, and what their plans are to expand in the future.

The Most Important Questions

- How many countries does your company do business in?

- What is the process to sponsor people internationally?
- Do you have to register in each country you want to sponsor people in?
- Are there any additional requirements to get paid on your international business volume?
- Does the company have the logistics and ability to service people in different countries?

My Best Suggestion

My best suggestion is to look for an MLM company that does business in at least 20-50 countries, and preferably more than that.

You also want a company with a presence in Africa and Asia. These two continents are a hotbed for MLM activity.

Final Thoughts

In conclusion, every large and successful MLM Company I know of has a strong international presence. While network marketing is a bit stagnant here in America, it continues to grow in popularity worldwide. Working with a company that doesn't operate internationally is a big mistake, as I see it.

Chapter 17: Your Intuition

After you've evaluated the different areas we talked about in this book, there is one final consideration: your intuition.

What does your gut say to you about the company? Deep down in your mind does it feel like a good deal to you or not? Would you be proud to be part of the company and share it with others?

Only you can decide that for yourself. A company might pass every other test I've included in this book, but if it doesn't pass the common sense or intuition test, I personally would not join.

I'll leave that up to you. Every time I have ever gone against my gut feeling, it has always come back to haunt me.

You might not be 100% sure the business is for you. That's actually quite normal. **Most people are skeptical of things they do not know much about.**

Do More Research

I believe it is smart to do your due diligence. I'm not just talking about doing a "Google" search either. Just because you read something online doesn't mean it's true. Anyone can publish a website posting something negative about anything they want.

If you are unsure about the company owners, call them. If you are unsure about the products, order them and try them out. If you are unsure if the business works, talk with three or four successful distributors and ask them your questions. If you are unsure about the compensation plan, take some time to study it.

Whatever you do, don't let ignorance keep you from joining a great opportunity. You owe it to yourself to at least get your questions answered before you make a decision.

Talk with Someone Successful in the Company

The person sharing the business with you might be brand new to the business, and not have all the answers. That's why I highly suggest you talk with one or more successful distributors in the company.

Ask them your questions, take some time to think over their answers and then make a decision.

Think about it this way for a minute. If you were going to buy a franchise, wouldn't you want to talk to three or four of their franchisees to see what their experience with the company has been like?

The last thing you want to do is ask you friends what they think. Why? Because they are unqualified to talk about the business.

If you needed your car fixed, would you talk to your friend who doesn't know anything about fixing cars, or would you consult with a trusted mechanic? <u>Be cautious who you get your advice from</u>.

Talk it Over with Your Spouse

I will tell you this. Opposites attract. For every 100 couples I approach, in only about 1 in 100 cases are

BOTH spouses excited about the business. Normally, one spouse is excited, or somewhat excited, and the other is negative or neutral. That is normal.

As a courtesy, you should have a discussion with your spouse about the business and products. Tell them WHAT interests you about the business and WHY you would consider it. Listen to their point of view. Ask them what they think.

Even though they may have a different viewpoint than you, you owe it to them to at least hear them out. Who knows, they might decide this business is the best thing since sliced bread, and it's something they would love to do with you.

If nothing else, you've at least included them in your decision-making process.

The Most Important Questions

- What is your gut saying to you about the business?
- Have you done your due diligence and got your questions answered before you made a decision?
- If you are skeptical, what makes you skeptical about the business?
- Is this a business you would be proud to be part of and share with your friends?

My Best Suggestion

Do your due diligence, ask tons of questions, talk with the company leadership team, try out some samples, talk with your spouse, sleep on it and then LISTEN TO YOUR INITUTION.

Final Thoughts

In review, listening to your intuition is vitally important. Just make sure you aren't too quick to come to a decision, without educating yourself first.

The last thing you want to do is be skeptical and turn down something that could completely change your life for the better, just because you were uninformed.

Part Three:

Picking a Company & Sponsor

Chapter 18: The 7-Step Process to Pick a Company & Sponsor

In this chapter, I'm going to talk about the process of choosing a network marketing company and finding a sponsor.

I have a 7-step process I've created to help people find the right company. I want to share this 7-step process with you, to help you get it right.

STEP # 1: Find a Product Line or Niche You Are Passionate About

You really want to choose a product line or niche you are passionate about and has mass market demand.

It's really hard to be successful doing something or selling something that you're not passionate about or don't believe in.

If you're someone who doesn't like skincare, as an example, do not join a skin care network marketing company.

Here's the first thing I suggest you do. Take ten minutes right now and brainstorm as many potential "niches" or "product lines" that interest you. Put some serious thought into this.

Some of the most common niches in our industry include:

- Weight Loss
- Skin Care
- Essential Oils

- Insurance & Investing
- Health & Wellness
- Beauty & Cosmetics
- Telecommunications
- Electricity
- Services
- Coffee
- Adult Toys

Once you come up with a master list, rank the niches from one to five. Place a # 1 next to the niche that excites you the most, a # 2 by the second one and so forth.

Whittle your list down to your top three choices. Once you've done that you can move to the next step.

Step # 2: Make a Detailed List of MLM Companies That Offer the Type of Product or Service You Want to Promote

The next thing you want to do is make a list of 5+ network marketing companies that offer the type of product or service you want to sell. You might have more options than that, maybe less. Aim to find minimum three companies.

Let's assume that your passion is weight loss. You're passionate about helping others lose weight and improve their health.

What I would do at this point is do a quick internet search for "weight loss MLM Companies." I would also visit the Direct Selling Association website to see what companies are listed there.

This is the brainstorming phase. The more potential companies you can come up with the better.

After you finish your list, pick the three to five companies that interest you the most and then move to the next step.

Step # 3: Compare Each Company on the 13 Criteria I Shared Earlier

The next step is to compare and analyze each company on the different criteria I shared with you earlier in this book. You want to look at:

- The Products or Services
- The Company's Track Record & Reputation
- The Compensation Plan
- Training & Systems
- Technology & Tools
- The Distributor Agreement
- The Start-Up & Ongoing Costs
- Timing
- The Company's Financials & Leadership Team
- Meetings, Events, Support & Culture
- Retailing vs. Recruiting
- International Markets & Expansion
- Your Intuition

The best way to do this is take out a sheet of paper. On the top of the paper, make a column for each company you want to evaluate. On the left side of the paper, write down these 13 things you want to compare.

Take some time and evaluate each network marketing company. Give it a score from 1-10 in each category. Add up the scores to get a final score.

Please keep in mind it might take you a week or two to complete these steps. You shouldn't rush it. You will have to research and investigate each company in each category.

Step # 4: Whittle Your List Down to Your Top Three Choices

After you've finished grading each network marketing company, whittle your list down to the top three choices. You don't necessarily have to pick the companies with the three highest scores, but you should.

After all, why even do this process if you aren't going to pick the company with the highest, or second highest score? Once you've whittled your list down to your top two or three choices you are ready for the next step.

Step # 5: Order Some Products

What I would recommend you do at this point is to become a retail customer with each of your top two or three companies.

You want to try out the products or services. Find out what you can about the products. Compare the prices, the quality, the ingredients, etc.

Share the products with family and friends. Get their input. See what they have to say. Research the products online. Find out what others are saying about the products.

Once you've been a customer for these different companies, I think it'll be pretty easy to choose the company you like best. If their products suck, why would you want to represent the company as a distributor?

On the other hand, if you absolutely love the products, you know you have your hands on something good. Chances are, one company's products will really stand out and your instincts will tell you which company to choose.

Once again, you've got to love the products, and the products must be a good deal for customers. The only way to know that is to be a customer first.

When you are a customer first, it lets you look at the products objectively. You're not attached to the business aspect of it.

It lets you determine if the products are a good value to people outside of the business, which is really important.

Step # 6: Pick the Best Company for You

Your next step is to pick the company that you like the best. You've done your research. You've been a customer for a few different network marketing companies. All you need to do now is pick the company that resonates with you the most.

Since you've already researched the company and sampled the products, this should be a fairly easy decision to make.

Step # 7: Pick a Good Sponsor

Once you find the company you want to join, the final step is to pick a sponsor.

Search online and find a few successful people in the company. Make a list of at least three to five potential sponsors. Start on YouTube or on the company's corporate website where they share their success stories.

You want to choose your sponsor just like you chose your company. You don't want your sponsor to choose you. You want to choose who you work with and team up with them. Ask them a lot of questions, such as:

- How long have you been in the company?
- What type of success have you achieved?
- How many people have you helped become successful?
- What rank are you in the company?
- What do you like about the company?
- What do you dislike about the company?
- What systems do you have in place?
- What will you do to help me?
- What type of meetings and training do you offer?
- How will we work together?

These are just a few questions you should ask your potential sponsor.

Once again, it's really important to team up with someone who's serious about their business and is willing to help you succeed. Also, you want someone you can get along with and trust.

Personally, I would interview at least three potential sponsors and then pick the one I thought would be the best fit.

One final consideration is upline support. In addition to your potential sponsor, how many people are there in the upline support team you can work with? The more the better.

The Most Important Questions

- Did I like the products?
- After doing my research does the company and business opportunity make sense?
- Have I found the right sponsor and upline support team to work with?

My Best Suggestion

Take your time and go through this complete process. You want to do it right the first time around. Treat this like you would if you were buying a million-dollar franchise.

Final Thoughts

In review, this is the 7-step process I recommend when choosing an MLM Company. If you follow this advice, you should find the right company and sponsor to work with.

It's not 100% guaranteed, but it's much more practical than just randomly picking a company or sponsor.

Chapter 19: Starting Over

There might come a point in your network marketing career when you have to start over. I hope this never happens to you. I hope you find the right opportunity the first time around and build your dynasty. For most people, it rarely works out that way.

Even after you do your due diligence, and follow the advice outlined in this book to choose the right opportunity, you never really know how "good" or "solid" the company will be until you've spent 12 to 36-months building your business.

Your experience can be like buying a car. You might love the car during the test drive, but after you drive it for a year, you realize it isn't what you thought it was. You might even find out you bought a LEMON.

You might be forced to sell your business, resign your position, switch to another network marketing company, or even leave the industry for good.

Why? Well, lots of crazy things can happen in business and life. Your spouse might divorce you and take your business as part of the settlement. You might lose interest in the industry altogether. You might decide to pursue other income streams. You might get sick.

The company's CEO or founder might die. The company might merge with another network marketing company. Perhaps your company gets sued and shuts down. Maybe the company changes its mission and focus.

Or, **the company gets greedy and changes the deal, drastically cutting commissions and payouts**. Unfortunately, this happens frequently in our industry. Normally, it starts with one small change. And then another. And then another change. Before you realize it, the company you are in now has nothing in common with what it was like when you first joined.

I will be the first to tell you that **you need to know when to cut your losses and move on**. However, jumping ship should never be your first option. That was a mistake I made several times in my own career, and I really regret it.

After all, you've probably spent several YEARS building up your residual income and customer base. You need to put in considerable thought before you make any decision.

If you decide that leaving is your only option, figure out if there is a way you can still collect the residual income from the team you've built, even if you distance yourself from the business. Or, figure out how to sell your business quickly and profitably so you can have a clean break.

I will leave you with this. <u>Change is inevitable.</u> **No matter what company you represent, there will always be changes.** You must embrace change, and realize that all people and companies must change to grow bigger and better.

Never make a big decision based on your raw emotions. Put some serious thought into your decision. Seek counsel. Pray about it. Meditate on it. Sleep on it.

And realize this, even if you have to start over again in a different opportunity at some point in the future, your skills and experience will put you in a position to achieve success much quicker the second time around!

Chapter 20: What Now?

Congratulations. You've finished the meat and potatoes in this book. You're probably wondering what you should do next. Here is what I suggest you do.

STEP # 1: Evaluate Your Current Situation

If you're not yet involved in this great industry, follow the advice in this book and start looking for a company.

On the other hand, if you're already a distributor, you need to decide if your current company is still a good fit for you. I would not be quick to jump ship, but I would put some serious thought into it.

Do you like the company's product line? Are you passionate about it? Does the company culture resonate with you?

Are you happy with your sponsor and upline? Do you feel like your business is moving forward and making progress, or will be in the near future?

If you are happy, stay put and keep building. If you're not happy with your current company, you might need to change companies.

Whatever you do, put some serious thought into it. **If you have any time invested in the company, I would be very slow to throw in the towel and leave.** Remember, the grass is greenest where you water it!

STEP # 2: Make a Decision

After you've evaluated your current situation, make a decision. By all means "sleep on it" or "pray about it" first.

Take whatever time is needed, make your decision and move forward, either with your current company or by finding a new one.

You will never have "all the facts". Do your due diligence, make an informed decision and never look back.

STEP # 3: Get to Work

The next step is to get to work. Assuming you've found a network marketing company you love, it's time to put on your blinders for the next three to five years and get to work.

Find a mentor, develop a game-plan, set some goals, create a work schedule and take massive action with your business. Do a few 90-day blitzes back-to-back to create some quick momentum in your business.

No matter what company you represent, you're going to have to buckle down, commit, and put in the work. You might not see big results right away, but if you stay persistent and consistent, your business will grow.

The Most Important Questions

- What are my goals for the next 90-days, six months and 12-months?
- What is my game-plan to make this happen?

- Who will be working with me throughout this process?

My Best Suggestion

Act as if you have one-million dollars invested in your business. Once you've found an MLM Company you love, create a game-plan and get to work. Put on your blinders for the next three to five years and don't look at other opportunities.

Final Thoughts

In conclusion, sometimes you need to start over. Things happen. If you have to start over at some point, you'll be okay. Many top earners have had to start over several times before eventually finding their forever home.

Final Thoughts

I would like to personally thank you for purchasing and reading my book *How to Find the Right Network Marketing Company.*

I hope you found the information helpful and I really hope you will follow the steps I provided to find the right MLM Company for yourself.

Choosing the right network marketing company at the right time is essential if you want long-term success in our industry. It's much better to start right than start over.

If you enjoyed the book, I would really appreciate if you took a few minutes and left a review on Amazon® for me. If you could be specific and talk about how the book helped you, that would be great.

In addition, I would love to connect with you and answer your questions. Feel free to send me an email to chuck@onlinemlmcommunity.com.

Thanks for your business. I appreciate it!

About Me

Chuck Holmes is a network marketing professional, blogger, author, entrepreneur and ambassador to the MLM Industry.

He's currently the top recruiter and top producer in his company, which specializes in natural and organic products.

Chuck is the webmaster and publisher of **OnlineMLMCommunity.com**, one of the most popular MLM blogs in the world. He spends his days reading and writing about the industry, and building his own team.

He is a former Army Major and combat veteran. He holds a Bachelor's Degree in Politics and a Master's Degree in Management. He is also a Certified Small Business Coach.

He resides in Homosassa, Florida with his wife, Rachel. He can be reached by email at chuck@onlinemlmcommunity.com.

Recommended Reading

Leaders are readers. Here are a few books that changed my life and business for the better. The titles are listed in alphabetical order.

1. *Acres of Diamonds* by Russell Conwell
2. *All You Can Do Is All You Can Do, But All You Can Do Is Enough* by A.L. Williams
3. *Beach Money* by Jordan Adler
4. *Bringing Out the Best in People* by Alan Loy Mcginnis
5. *Go Pro! How to Be a Network Marketing Professional* by Eric Worre
6. *Guerrilla Multi-Level Marketing* by Jay Conrad Levinson
7. *How I Raised Myself from Failure to Success in Selling* by Frank Bettger
8. *How to Win Friends & Influence People* by Dale Carnegie
9. *Recruit & Grow Rich* by David Ward
10. *Rich Dad, Poor Dad* by Robert Kiyosaki
11. *Secrets of the Millionaire Mind* by T. Harv Eker
12. *Six Figures in Six Months* by Clay Stevens
13. *The 45-Second Presentation* by Don Failla

14. *The Dream Giver* by Bruce Wilkinson

15. *The E-Myth Revisited* by Michael Gerber

16. *The Five Love Languages* by Dr. Gary Chapman

17. *The Four-Hour Work Week* by Tim Ferris

18. *The Four-Year Career®* by Richard Bliss Brooke

19. *The Greatest Networker in the World* by John Milton Fogg

20. *The Magic of Thinking Big* by Dr. David Schwarz

21. *The Total Money Makeover* by Dave Ramsey

22. *Think & Grow Rich* by Napoleon Hill

23. *Your Best Year in Network Marketing* by Mark Yarnell

Let's Work Together!

I would like to formally welcome you to partner up with me in my MLM Company. It specializes in natural and organic products.

I've gone through each step in this book to evaluate the company, before I got involved. Needless to say, I am very happy and am quickly moving my way up through the ranks.

If you want to work with a successful mentor, in the right company at the right time, I would like to invite you to take a look at what I have to offer you. To learn more, simply visit my website:

www.StartaFunBiz.com

Your information is never shared or sold. You can unsubscribe at any time, if you decide it isn't a good fit for you. Also, feel free to send me an email to **chuck@onlinemlmcommunity.com**.

I look forward to hearing from you.

www.ingramcontent.com/pod-product-compliance
Lightning Source LLC
Chambersburg PA
CBHW071036240526
45469CB00006BD/2230